it only hurts between paydays

AMY ROSS YOUNG

ACCENT BOOKS
Denver, Colorado

Scripture quotations are taken from *The New Scofield Reference Bible,* Authorized King James Version. Copyright © 1967 by Oxford University Press, Inc. Used by permission.

ACCENT BOOKS
12100 W. Sixth Avenue
P.O. Box 15337
Denver, Colorado 80215

Copyright © 1975 B/P Publications, Inc.

Printed in U.S.A.

Library of Congress Catalog Card Number: 75-17366

ISBN 0-916406-09-1

Dedication

This book is dedicated . . .

To the real "Mike" and "Lynn," for letting me share in the joy of their financial victory.

To both sets of parents who helped by *not* helping as Mike and Lynn learned to live by the bright red budget book; for their prayerful support—and for remaining my friends through it all.

To all young marrieds who are in financial trouble. My sincere prayer is that they will find something in this book to start them on the road to recovery.

To all young couples about to be married. May they find direction for starting right and avoiding the pitfalls of financial mismanagement.

Appreciation

My Sincere Thanks . . .

To two friends and pastors, Dr. Earle E. Matteson and Dr. Hubert Verrill for their wise and helpful counsel.

To Haskal Gallimore and Paul Riley for their professional research and advice.

To my friend and co-worker, Violet T. Pearson, for patiently "listening" after each chapter was written, and for her expert editing of the completed manuscript.

And last, but not least, to my friend and Boss, Dr. Robert L. Mosier for demanding my best and then trusting me to do it.

Amy Ross Young

Contents

Chapter One
One Question—And I Was Involved 7

Chapter Two
Ouch! The Sting of Reality 13

Chapter Three
Is It a Tithe—Or Nothing? 21

Chapter Four
Meet Your Bright Red Budget Book 29

Chapter Five
Its Name Is Credit Card 41

Chapter Six
Learning to Say, "I Can't Afford It" 47

Chapter Seven
Just Between Us Girls and That Friendly
Supermarket 55

Chapter Eight
Aiming at Goals, One, Two and Three 63

Chapter Nine
The Unseen Dollars Behind Your Dream House 73

Chapter Ten
Looking For Alternatives Can Be Fun 83

Chapter Eleven
A Sane Approach to Your Insurance Needs 91

Chapter Twelve
The Joy of a Bill Marked "Paid" 101

Chapter Thirteen
Cutting The Budget Pie Into Pieces 107

Chapter Fourteen
Who Promised You a Rose Garden? 117

Chapter Fifteen
Now That You're Finally Out of Debt! 123

"Let your manner of life be without covetousness, and be content with such things as ye have . . ."
Hebrews 13:5

CHAPTER ONE

One Question —and I Was Involved

Mike and Lynn were two terrific young people with a shaky five-year marriage, a three-year old son—and problems. All kinds of problems, one of which was the inability to manage their personal finances. Now, projecting sales, cost analysis, controlling inventory and keeping an eye on department budgets is a way of life for me. I'm in the habit of solving problems every day. Hearing Mike describe his financial dilemma created a reflex action in me.

I didn't set out to get involved. It just happened as the result of one well-meaning question.

"Mike, would you like some help organizing your finances?"

That's all it took.

With a catch in his voice, this heart-broken young six-footer quietly said, "I could sure use some."

Afraid he might change his mind, I asked, "When can we get together?"

"How about tomorrow evening?" he replied.

This was the beginning of a togetherness you may find hard to believe.

Mike's parents have been close friends of mine for many years, and Lynn's folks are friends of more recent days. I am "Aunt Amy" to little Bobby. We were all concerned about Mike and Lynn. For several months the tension between them was evident. The closeness—the oneness, was gone.

Being aware of this, we were still not prepared for Mike's phone call asking his folks if he could move back home—just until he and Lynn could reach a decision regarding their future. Lynn and little Bobby were going to stay in the apartment.

Mike was like one of my own, and I was sharing the shock of this news with both families. Having just read that 75 per cent of all broken marriages could be traced to money problems, I decided to stick my neck out—or my nose in.

This conversation between Mike and me took place in my car as we drove toward a cheery, sunny restaurant on the outskirts of town where we were to meet his parents and young son for Sunday dinner.

He and Lynn had been separated for one short, agonizing week. His initial anger was exhausted. All that remained was the deep hurt and feeling of failure and defeat.

When we arrived at the restaurant, Bobby flung himself into his daddy's arms—and held on. He was not too young to know that something was not right with his little world. During dinner, we all made a sterling effort to match the mood of our surroundings. The cheery atmosphere seemed to mock us. We talked all around the one question uppermost in our thoughts: "Was this young family, so dear to us, doomed to divorce?"

As we walked to the parking lot, I asked Mike to bring every scrap of information he might have regarding their finances with him the following evening. Little did I realize what I was asking for, but the Lord knew and graciously led each step of the way in the months to come.

Driving home, along the country road, I began to think about Mike, Lynn—and money. Could this really be at the bottom of their separation—or was it a symptom of a more basic problem? Were 75 per cent of all divorces actually due to disagreements over the dollar? Or, could money mismanagement just be the tangible evidence of an intangible weakness in the marriage structure?

A young couple with opposing purposes in life, an inability to communicate, and a failure to exercise self-discipline in their personal finances—is headed for trouble. If they separate, money problems will be blamed.

On the other hand, a young couple with a common goal, who can discuss their problems, and who know how to control their personal finances, can face the most devastating money crisis—together—and come out on top.

When the almighty dollar causes problems in your marriage, you can fight and run—or, you can stand together and fight your way out. It is your choice.

When Mike and Lynn saw a balanced budget replacing the maze of their indebtedness, they began to talk about the need for a simple and practical help for young couples just starting out. And for those who are already in financial trouble.

They encouraged me to tell their story and set forth the plan we used in working out their problems—not all of them past-due bills!

We will leave their story at times to cover subjects they felt should be included, such as, how to look at tithing during a financial crisis; how credit cards should be used; goal setting as a way of life; costs to be considered when buying a house; how to control the grocery budget; a sane approach to life insurance and the value of percentage budgeting.

Let me be the first to admit that this is not a highly technical, or sophisticated budget plan. But it is not aimed at solving the problems of highly technical and sophisticated budgets. It isn't geared to the fiscal policies of large corporations; it is geared to the financial plight of young marrieds with aching checkbooks and sagging spirits.

Also, this book is not written for those who are in control of their personal finances and have a good working system. It is written for "beginners," and those who need help and encouragement in getting control and learning to live within the limits of their income. Built into this easy-to-use plan is the fun, or self-satisfaction, of watching your progress from payday to payday.

The real "Mike" and "Lynn" join me in prayer that God will use our experience to bless and enrich the lives of countless others with a need similar to theirs.

CHAPTER TWO

Ouch!
The Sting
of Reality

Mike and I sat facing each other across my dining room table that first Monday evening—and between us lay that ominous pile of bills. Sometimes it is easier to run from reality than it is to face it, but running from a problem never solves it.

"Where do we begin?" Mike wanted to know, a note of discouragement in his voice.

Determined to be optimistic, I gave him a cheery smile and replied, "Just give me the facts."

If you have more bills than you can pay, this is the place to begin. Face the facts. All of them. Start with a blank piece of paper and at the top list your take-home pay for each payday in the month. These are the "assets" with which you have to work.

Next, list your "liabilities," everything you owe. There should be nothing left uncovered at this point. Expose every financial commitment you have.

That's precisely what Mike and I did. First, his assets—money to use. Second, his liabilities—for starters that pile of monthly statements on the table! We ended up with one car payment; a monthly insurance premium; seven past-due charge accounts, and a list of doctor bills that looked like the first page in "Who's Who in the AMA."

By now it was too late to run. I was hooked. This was going to be as much of a challenge to me as an over-sized bone is to an under-sized dog.

It would have been great if all of Mike's take-home pay could have been applied to those past-due bills, but the usual monthly living expenses had to be added to the list.

There was rent on the apartment (you may have a house payment), utilities, telephone bill, gasoline for the car, grocery money for Lynn and Bobby and some spending money for Mike. Your list will not be too different.

"Mike," I said, "it is pretty bad. Are you sure you want me involved in this?"

"Sure," he gulped. "I can't do it alone."

Even Mike and I, together, couldn't do it. But, we both knew Someone who could give us the wisdom and the strength to gain control of this situation. Two verses of Scripture came to mind. "I can do all things through Christ, who strengtheneth me" (Philippians 4:13), and "If any of you lack wisdom, let him ask of God, who giveth to all men liberally, and upbraideth not; and it shall be given him"

(James 1:5). We stopped and asked the Lord to do just that.

After you have completed your list of debts and monthly living expenses, you have a glimpse of reality, but don't stop there. That isn't the basic problem. You need to look the "reason" for your financial dilemma straight in the eye.

"Mike," I asked, "what do you think has gotten your finances in this condition?"

After a few attempts to skirt the issue, he admitted, "Just charging faster than we could pay, I guess."

It was out in the open. We both started to laugh, for it was a rather obvious conclusion. Then, I did something I would never have dared do if I had given it that famous "second thought."

"Would you like me to take possession of your charge cards for the duration?"

To my amazement, he said, "Fine," and before I could apologize for being so presumptuous, he was dealing charge cards out of his billfold as if that were the brightest idea he had heard all evening.

"Wow! You went too far," you are probably saying about now.

It was an extreme measure, but the Lord was leading, for it later proved to be an excellent budget balancer and a marriage saver, too.

If you, like Mike and Lynn, have been charging faster than you can pay, there is only one way to correct the problem. Stop charging! And, start paying. It is as simple as that. Call a moratorium on buying—until everything you have been charging is paid for.

Perhaps you can resist the urge to add to those convenient charge accounts—and I hope you can.

But, when the pressure is really on, it might help if someone else were in possession of *your* charge cards.

The reason behind your shortage of funds may not be charge accounts. Some people can't pass up the opportunity to buy on the installment plan. A middle-aged couple I knew was making four major installment payments a month and trying to keep up with several very active charge accounts at the same time. The end result—they sold their home, paid the bills and got a divorce. You may even find that without charge accounts and installment payments, your money runs through your fingers like water. You have nothing in particular to show for it. It just seems to disappear.

Whatever the reason, it is important to think it through, recognize it for what it is, and face the problem straight on. Then, and only then, will you be ready to find a solution.

A solution is what Mike and I were trying to find. When we finished listing every financial item he had, it looked like this:

CHARGE ACCOUNTS

Department Store #1	$ 480
Department Store #2	413
Department Store #3	200
Oil Company #1	440
Oil Company #2	200
Master Charge	350
BankAmericard	700
Total	$2,783

MONTHLY EXPENSES

Rent	$120
Utilities	15

Telephone	8
Groceries	100
Gasoline	50
Insurance	12
Car Payment	125
Total	$430

YEARLY EXPENSES

Car License	$ 40
Car Insurance	150
Income Tax Service	25
Total	$215

MEDICAL EXPENSES

Doctor Bills	$1,000

Mike's finances were definitely in control of him! It would be exciting to reverse this situation and put *him* in control. From the look on Mike's face, however, he was not sharing my anticipation. Somehow, that look of defeat, discouragement and doubt had to be turned into something better.

"All right," I said, "let's begin to organize this mess."

Mike replied, "This I've got to see!"

When your initial list is complete, you are ready to divide it up and build a payment schedule. I prefer the twice-monthly budget plan, using the 1st and 15th of each month as the budget dates. The dates are not as important as the "schedule." Mike and Lynn obviously had not been following any sort of financial schedule, or plan. And, if you are in the same condition, you probably have not had one either.

Mike and Lynn's story could have been completely different if they had worked out a financial plan before they got married, instead of after they were up to their ears in debt. If you are planning on getting married, you can use this plan and build a budget for your anticipated living expenses, any debts you might bring into the marriage, and also a savings plan for the future.

This bit of counsel may be too late for you. If it is, follow along with Mike and gain control of your personal pile of bills.

We were ready to begin a rough draft of Mike's proposed payment schedule. He wrote, "December 1st," at the top of a clean sheet of paper, and added, "December 15th," about half-way down.

"Let's make your giving to the Lord the first item under both dates," I suggested.

Mike hesitated. "Wel-l-l, we haven't been able to tithe, so we haven't been giving anything," he admitted. "But, I would like to start."

Mike's remark opened up a subject that needed careful handling. Before we discussed how much he should give, I needed time to pray, study and talk it over with wiser heads than mine. Mike didn't need to be confused at this late hour. And besides, the sting of all this reality was enough for one night.

We decided to meet again on Friday—the day before his next payday. We would build his budget and pay his first round of bills.

CHAPTER THREE

Is It a Tithe —Or Nothing?

Trying to find the right guidance for Mike before Friday night started me thinking. Why do people tithe? This has always fascinated me and the results of my research were eye-opening. However, I hope that by the time you finish reading this chapter we will have moved from the eyes to the heart.

One teenager was experiencing some expensive problems with her car. Her somewhat angry reaction was, "I've been tithing! I thought God was supposed to keep things like this from happening!"

This is not too different from the adult who said, "I'm afraid not to tithe. I know that if I don't, something terrible and expensive will happen."

Tithing in these two cases falls into the category

of buying "accident insurance," or is it "health insurance?" There is little joy in this kind of giving.

Next, I ran into a financially-wise, money-minded tither. "I figure I might as well give it to the church as to the government." To him it is an excellent tax deduction.

Then, there was the good-guy-with-the-white-hat tither. "I try to do what's right . . . and, I give to the church." He thinks his good deeds and giving are just the price of a one-way ticket to Heaven.

Sad? Yes, but I'm happy to report that these were in the minority. Let me tell you about an experience I recently had with my little 81 year old mother. I believe she represents the majority of tithing Christians who give because they love the Lord and feel it is their privilege and responsibility to give back to God a portion of what He has given to them.

Mother is almost blind and can no longer enjoy reading for herself. One day as I walked through the door of her apartment, she handed me some papers, along with her mail.

"What's this?" she wanted to know.

Glancing at the papers, I replied, "It's information about the Faith Promise program at your church."

"Yes, I know that, but isn't there something I'm supposed to fill out?"

She was right. There was a card on which she was to list the amount of her faith promise. Mother faithfully tithes her limited income, and when her monthly pension check arrives in the mail, this is the first check she wants me to write. She frequently reminds me, "This is my tithe. What I put in Sunday School is my offering to the Lord." I guess I just didn't expect her to do more.

She loves to tell how during the depression my

father wouldn't let her tithe. When he died several years later, she tithed his insurance money—and she firmly ends the story with, "And, I've been tithing ever since!"

We filled out the Faith Promise card. I suggested $3, but she said, "No, make it $5."

Mother is not tithing to keep trouble from her door. She has had more than her share. And, at her age, income tax is the least of her worries. She is too smart to think she can buy her way into Heaven. She feels it is the least she can do to show her love for God and live in obedience to His Word. I'm sure it just never occurs to her to do otherwise.

Of all the people I talked to, the most heartbreaking were the young couples, like Mike and Lynn, who found themselves floundering in the quicksand of financial mismanagement. Almost without exception, they admitted that since they couldn't tithe—they were giving nothing. This is the group of people I want most to help.

Now, any research on tithing, or giving to the Lord, would be grossly incomplete without going to God's Word to see what it reveals on the subject. I decided to approach it the same way. Why did people in the Bible tithe?

The first reference I could find to the tithe was in Genesis 14. During the battle between the four kings from the North and the five kings of the South—Lot ended up a POW. When Abram heard the news about his nephew, he took 318 trained men and, gathering some friends along the way, set out to rescue Lot.

In a surprise night attack, Abram defeated the enemies and brought back all the goods that were taken from Sodom—and Lot, too! On his way home, Abram was met by the king of Sodom who came out to thank him for his deliverance. He also wanted to reward Abram by letting him keep all the goods he had retrieved.

But, Abram said, "No, thanks."

Another king also met Abram. His name was Melchizedek and he was not only king of Salem, but a priest of "the most High God." He brought food and refreshment for Abram and the weary men with him.

And—he blessed Abram. Genesis 14:20 tells us that " . . . he [Abram] gave him [Melchizedek] tithes of all."

There was no law that said Abram had to give a tithe to Melchizedek. He didn't do it to receive a blessing. He already had that. I think he recognized the superior position of this unusual priest/king and through him expressed his praise to God and gratitude for His blessing.

I turned over a few pages in my Bible to Genesis, Chapter 28, and ran into Abraham's grandson, Jacob. He had just been blessed by his father, Isaac, and sent to the land of his uncle in search of a wife. He stopped along the way for a night's rest and while he slept he had a dream. In the dream God spoke to Jacob and promised him some rather staggering blessings.

Jacob's reaction, upon waking, was a bit surprising. He started with a list of conditions for God. He said, "If God will be with me, and will keep me in this way that I go, and will give me bread to eat, and raiment to put on, so that I come again to my father's house in peace; then shall the Lord be my God."

He ends with this bargain: " . . . and of all that thou

shalt give me I will surely give the tenth unto thee."

Jacob wanted all the good things in life—first! Then, he would give the tenth of all he had to the Lord. God did bless Jacob just as He had promised, but He also let him experience some real problems along the way. Are you beginning to notice that our current day people bear a striking similarity to those recorded in the Bible?

When God gave the law to Moses, He included tithing as a part of Israel's worship and responsibility. In Numbers 18:25,26, the Lord instructs Moses regarding the tithe. The Levites were to take a tithe from the children of Israel as their inheritance from the Lord. They, in turn, were to offer "a tenth part of the tithe," in the form of a heave offering unto the Lord.

The children of Israel could not choose to—or not to—tithe. It was required by law. Nor, could they bargain with God. Who am I kidding? You only have to read Malachi, Chapter 3, to discover that at least part of Israel had stopped tithing.

God asked, "Will a man rob God?"

When they replied, "How have we robbed thee?" God answered, "In tithes and offerings." Malachi 3:7 indicates that their lack of giving was a result of being away from God.

I can almost hear you murmur, "But we Christians are not under law. We are under grace." And, of course, you are right. In fact, we could put it another way. We are not under law—we are under love! What Israel tried to do to obey God's law, we *want* to do because of Christ's love for us—and our love for Him. It was because of His love that He did what man was unable to do. In Matthew 5:17, Jesus said, "Think not that I am come to destroy the law. . . I am not come to destroy, but to fulfill."

There is little said about tithing in the New Testament. The first mention is in Matthew 23:23. Jesus is rebuking the scribes and Pharisees: "Woe unto you, scribes and Pharisees, hypocrites! For ye pay tithe of mint and anise and cummin, and have omitted the weightier matters of the law, justice, mercy and faith; these ought ye to have done, and not to leave the other undone." Verse 28 wraps up their problem: "Even so ye also outwardly appear righteous unto men, but within ye are full of hypocrisy and iniquity."

The most important question we have to answer is, "Do we have a right heart relationship with the Lord Jesus Christ?" If we do, our giving will not be a problem.

We are not left to wonder, however, about the New Testament pattern of giving. In I Corinthians 16:2 we read, "Upon the first day of the week let every one of you lay by him in store as God hath prospered him." What can we learn from this? We are to be *regular* in our giving. *Every* Christian is to give and the amount is to be *in proportion* to our prosperity. These are all outward manifestations.

Paul gets down to the "heart" of giving in II Corinthians, Chapter 8. He is dealing with the giving to be used to help the poor in the church at Jerusalem. The Corinthians were a bit lackadaisical in doing their part.

Would you get your Bible and read verses 7 through 12? I will just list the main points. In verse 7, " . . . see that ye abound in this grace also." In verse 8, " . . . to prove the sincerity of your love." In verse 11, " . . . a performance also out of that which ye have."

Verse 12 tells us that we are to have a "willing mind," and that if we do, " . . . it is accepted according to that which a man hath, and not according to that which he hath not." There it is. Giving is a grace. It should abound in our lives—out of a sincere love and a willing mind.

I would like to go back to the financially burdened young couples, those in the middle of a crisis, who feel they must give a tenth—or nothing. There are two kinds of financial crises. First, is the one over which you have absolutely no control. It is just not your fault! It might be the loss of a job; a serious illness with the accompanying medical expenses; the death of the husband, or wife; a fire; an accident. We could go on, but you get the idea.

Second, is the kind that is self-inflicted. A crisis which you have created. I recently heard of one young couple who falls into this category. Within six months, they had purchased a new home, a new car—and a new boat! Could it be that they were trying to keep up with the Grodonovichs?

If you have created your own financial problem, you have moved away from God's perfect will for your life. Somehow your priorities have gotten out of focus, or it may have been poor judgment that got you where you are.

Take the first step to regain control of your money. Follow along with Mike and Lynn and plan your recovery. Then, with a willing heart, give God the "first part" of your income. He doesn't expect you to give what you do not have, but He does expect you to prove the sincerity of your love—by giving what you can.

The tithe is every Christian's responsibility before God. Make it your goal.

CHAPTER FOUR

Meet Your Bright Red Budget Book

It was Friday night and promptly at 7:30, Mike rang the doorbell. He was smiling, but his eyes and his greeting revealed what was going on inside.

"Hi! Here comes your walking disaster area!"

I laughed and replied, "Come on in. We'll have to fix that."

As soon as he was inside, he perked up and, with his nose in the air, asked, "What's that I smell?"

I was glad for the aroma of those just-baked chocolate chip cookies!

Once again Mike and I faced each other across my dining room table. Picking up the bright red, three-ringed notebook purchased earlier in the week, I said, "Mike, meet your new budget book."

With mock respect, he nodded his head and responded, "Greetings! You realize that I am expecting a miracle out of you!"

Looking him straight in the eye, I said, "No, Mike, we are expecting a miracle out of YOU."

This budget book that we are introducing to you is practical and even fun, but it is an inanimate object with no power to straighten out your money problems. It's all up to you. The book contains the plan, but you have to work it.

There are three things—make it four—you will need to implement this simple plan for financial recovery. First, if you do not already have one, you need a joint checking account. Second, a "bright red" budget book. We are using a standard 9×7-inch, three-ring binder; 8½×5½-inch ruled ledger paper and two 9 × 6-inch manila envelopes punched to fit the notebook. Third—and fourth—you will need the complete cooperation of both husband and wife, and an instant dose of self-discipline.

A conveniently located bank will help you with the first requirement and your friendly stationery store will supply number two. You cannot, however, purchase the third and fourth necessity for any amount of money. These, you both have to want sincerely enough to work them out—together.

I opened Mike's new budget book so he could see how it was going to work. The first page was headed, "Yearly Expenses." These are the once-a-year bills that sneak up on you and play havoc with your regular monthly payment schedule. By listing them in the front of your budget book, you will be able to plan for them ahead of time. They will be included in the proper month for payment. This eliminates those surprise attacks!

Mike had only three such items to consider. Here is how his page appeared:

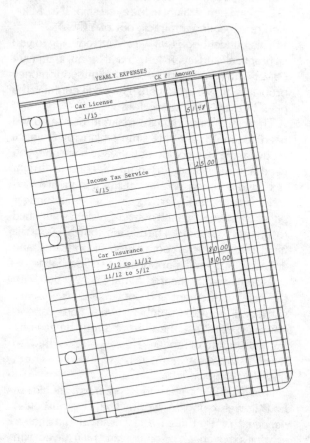

YEARLY EXPENSES	CK #	Amount
Car License 1/15		51 48
Income Tax Service 4/15		25 00
Car Insurance 5/12 to 11/12 11/12 to 5/12		80 00 80 00

We turned to the second page in Mike's book. I had some good news for him and decided to start with it.

"Mike, since you get paid every two weeks and we are setting your budget up on a twice-monthly schedule, you will have two pay checks a year that will be free and clear."

As I expected, anything that was going to be free and clear sounded great to Mike!

If you are one of the fortunate people who get paid every week, or every two weeks, it is still wise to cope with your monthly bills and living expenses on definite dates, such as the 1st and the 15th. There is, however, something you need to watch. Just because there are three paydays within one month does not mean that one of them is extra. Deciding which paychecks you can consider free and clear, takes a little planning. Let me show you what I mean.

Page two in Mike's budget book was titled, "Payday/Budget Date Schedule." Starting with his first payday in the new year, we listed every other Saturday for the remainder of the year. Then, we matched "budget dates" to the nearest payday to discover where the extra checks would fall.

Notice that in each case the payday, right after the "free" check, falls three days behind the budget date. (See 5/3 and 10/18.) In the month of May it took two paydays to get the schedule back into step. In October, it only took one payday to recover the three days' loss.

Be careful to work the schedule clear through to the end of the year—and don't take that extra check too soon! This guarantees that on the 1st and the 15th you will have the money in your checking account to cover your budget. It also allows for advance planning as to how you want to spend, or save, that free-and-clear paycheck.

Here's how Mike's schedule came out:

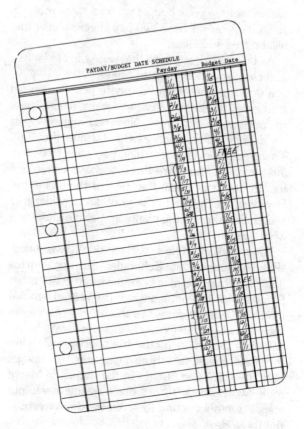

If you don't get paid every two weeks, don't despair. The basic principles of the rest of the budget book are for you. The important thing is what you do with your paycheck when you do get it!

Before we look at the next section in the budget book, we need to return to our work sheet and build a payment schedule. This takes a lot of erasing and juggling, so wait until it is "firmed-up" before putting it in your book.

Last Monday night, Mike had ended with a clean sheet of paper with "December 1st" and "December 15th" written on it. He was ready to launch the next phase in his drive toward good money management.

Since Mike was hoping to tithe, we listed this as the first item under both dates. Next, we listed the monthly living expenses. Some, like groceries and gasoline for the car, would appear every payday. It took careful planning to decide under which date the other payments would fall. The car payment had to be made early in the month, so it was placed under the "1st." This meant that the rent, also due on the 1st, would have to come out of the "15th" schedule for payment two weeks later. One paycheck would not handle both.

Next, and using only the minimum amounts required, we tried to fit those seven charge account payments into this new budget. Mike whipped out his little calculator and added up the two schedules. You guessed it! There was no way that Mike's take-home pay would cover those bills. Is it any wonder their marriage was in trouble?

"What do we do now?" Mike looked horrified.

Let me point out that there were no luxuries, nor even many of the necessities, included in this budget. It was bare bones! To hold to it was going to take extreme personal discipline on the part of both Mike and Lynn. It was time to share my research on tithing.

When we finished, I said, "Mike, the Lord knows and understands the mess you are in. You have already asked His forgiveness for your part in creating this crisis. He will honor you for trying to meet the demands of your creditors and rebuild your Christian testimony in this area."

He looked a bit puzzled. "What are you suggesting?" he asked.

"At this early point in your financial recovery, there are not enough dollars to go around," I explained. "The amount of your giving will have to be lowered."

We cut the tithe to about one third of a tithe. We agreed this was temporary. As the bills are cleared, the amount for the Lord will increase.

You may be facing the same struggle. You, too, want to tithe, but there is just no way! Can I challenge you to determine what you *can* give and make it the first item on your budget? Don't let it be a "tithe or nothing" decision.

With the amount of Mike's giving adjusted we were able to fit a payment on each of the seven charge accounts into the budget. Now we were ready to tie down the schedule in Mike's new book.

Here's the next step. Right after the first two pages (Yearly Expenses and Payday/Budget Date), place a colored divider labeled, "Payment Schedules." This can be made out of construction paper cut one-fourth inch wider than your ledger paper. In this section you will list the payment schedules for the 1st and 15th of every month in the current year. Unless your list is extremely long, you can have both paydays on one page.

Since Mike's future was so unsettled, we decided to do only one month at a time. He could add the rest of the year later.

It was time to pay bills!

The first check Mike wrote was made out to the

church—his first step to faithful, consistent giving. As each check was written, Mike placed a check mark beside the amount on the budget page. When the last check was sealed in its envelope, ready to be mailed *after* Mike deposited his paycheck, he heaved a satisfied sigh and said, "Man, that's a good feeling."

Here is how his first completed schedule looked:

December 1st			
	Church	✓	15 00
	Car payment	✓	125 00
	Groceries (Lynn-Bobby)	*	40 00
	Gasoline	*	25 00
	Insurance	✓	11 15
	Mike (Spending money)	*	20 00
	BankAmericard	✓	37 00
	Master Charge	✓	18 00
	Oil Company #1	✓	50 00
	Oil Company #2	✓	15 00
	Doctor #1	✓	5 00
			361 15
15th	Church		15 00
	Rent		120 00
	Groceries		40 00
	Gasoline		25 00
	Mike		20 00
	Telephone		8 00
	Utilities		15 00
	Department Store #1		50 00
	Department Store #2		20 00
	Department Store #3		35 00
	Doctor #2		10 00
			358 00

This provides a very practical way of keeping track of your expenses and a visual method of knowing when something is not paid. Since no charge cards will be used, and no checks written between paydays, the three items with an asterisk (*) will require cash. Mike will deposit all but $85 of his paycheck. This amount will have to cover those three items in the budget until next payday.

This is where self-discipline enters the picture. Just in case some of these "guidelines" slipped right by you, I'll recap them. Write *all* checks the night *before* payday. Have them ready to mail the minute your deposit is in the bank—even if they are early. This won't hurt your credit rating! It also helps control the temptation to hold back on maybe "just one payment." Let's call it the "deposit your check and pay bills fast" theory!

There is one more section in your budget book. The first is practical—this one is fun. The divider is labeled, "Record of Progress." Mike's first page in this part is headed, "Record of Giving." He listed the date, check number and the amount of his first check made out to the church. As paydays roll around he will have the satisfaction of watching the total grow—and at the end of the year he will have accurate records for his income tax report.

Each of the next seven pages represents one of those past-due bills. The name of the charge account is at the top of the page. The "starting balance" is at the right. Each time a payment is made, the new "finance charge" will be added to the old balance. The current payment can then be deducted. Remember, your finance charges are "deductible," on next year's income tax report.

The challenge, and yes, even fun, of this record of your own progress will soon have *you* hooked. You will be looking forward to next payday—so you can deduct more payments and see those balances decline. Controlling your finances will soon become automatic.

Here are Mike's first entries in his "Record of Progress."

OIL COMPANY #2			
Date	Fin.Chg.	Payment	Balance
Starting balance			200 00
12/1	2 27	15 00	187 27

OIL COMPANY #1			
Date	Fin.Chg.	Payment	Balance
Starting balance			440 00
12/1	4 96	50 00	394 96

MASTER CHARGE			
Date	Fin.Chg.	Payment	Balance
Starting balance			350 00
12/1	5 68	18 00	337 68

BANKAMERICARD			
Date	Fin.Chg.	Payment	Balance
Starting balance			700 00
12/1	11 05	37 00	674 05

All that is left are those two manila envelopes, punched to fit. Mark one, the "1st" and the other, the "15th." Put them in the front, or the back, of your budget book. As your statements arrive, place them in the proper envelope, along with other payment information needed. On payday, they are ready and waiting!

I must add that what else you include in your personal budget book is only limited by your imagination. I'm a "record-keeper." I keep a list of charge card numbers; checking and savings account numbers; a record of all major purchases—and a graph of my weight! Whatever you add to yours, have fun!

When Mike had finished deducting his payments he looked up with a smile and declared, "This is going to be fun!" What did I tell you? The look of discouragement, defeat and doubt was gone. Mike was still in debt—and he still had all of his other problems. But, now there was hope. He could see where he was going. It wasn't going to be easy, but the unknown factor in his finances had disappeared.

We closed the bright red budget book with satisfaction and an impatient anticipation for next payday. We agreed to meet again in two weeks and tackle the payment schedule for the 15th. Before Mike left for home, we sat back and enjoyed tall glasses of cold milk and those just-baked cookies.

Yes, we were going to have fun—at least on paydays. In between was going to hurt for a while!

CHAPTER FIVE

Its Name Is Credit Card

After Mike left, I sat for awhile thinking back over the evening. I couldn't get those seven charge accounts out of my mind. The minimum monthly payments amounted to $218. And, of that amount, $44 went for finance charges.

How could two intelligent Christian young people get so involved in credit buying? And, yet I knew they were not the exception to the rule. Too many of their friends were living the same way.

Could it be that young people are not aware of God's principles regarding money? I picked up my Bible and started looking for familiar passages on this subject.

Matthew 6:24-34 says it so beautifully. This

portion starts out, "No man can serve two masters; for either he will hate the one, and love the other; or else he will hold to the one, and despise the other. Ye cannot serve God and money."

Verses 25-32 teach what the Christian's attitude should be toward the physical and material *things* in life. We are not to be concerned about them. They are not to sidetrack us from the more vital part of life. Verse 33 makes it plain. "But seek ye first the kingdom of God, and his righteousness, and all these things shall be added unto you."

It's a matter of priorities.

Could it be that the bombardment of advertising urging children, young people and adults to buy—buy—buy, is drowning out the sound of God's call to put Him first?

There is one television commercial that makes it sound so easy:

"Our credit card will extend your income. Just buy what you want, when you want it. You can pay for it all at once—or a little at a time."

The product they are selling is a credit card. It is a small piece of plastic, approximately 3½ inches by 2 inches in size. It has been carefully designed to fit your billfold. A highly computerized system has assigned it a number.

I just took a quick look at some of mine and they are even attractive. One is gold and white; another red, white and blue. Each one has my name pressed right into the plastic. Credit cards are personal—and also very convenient.

If you are a member of the card-carrying class, you can purchase all of your gasoline from your favorite oil company with a credit card. You never have to be concerned about having cash when your tank runs dry.

You can even walk into a department store with only a few coins in your pocket and walk out, a few minutes later, with a new suit or dress. All you have to do is present your card and add your signature to the charge slip.

By now, you are probably wondering if I am building a case against credit cards. I'm not. They are attractive, personal and convenient. But—they are just what their name implies. Cards which allow you to "buy now and pay later." And, pay later you must! By ANY name, they are NOT another kind of money.

Working with Mike, and talking with other young couples, I have discovered that they are victims of the times in which we live. They have been convinced that they can buy almost anything they want—with a little magic credit card. Many families are charging themselves right into bankruptcy. Or—like Mike and Lynn, into the battle of their lives as they try to pay off the charges that were so easy to incur.

Credit cards, to be helpful, should be used—but never abused. If you can't pay the full amount when that monthly statement arrives, you are abusing it. Perhaps you are thinking, "Then, why is there the minimum payment on the statement, if the store expects me to pay the total due?"

The store doesn't expect you to, nor even want you to. A major part of their profit depends on your doing just the opposite. One national chain of stores is reported to have said that they would have to go out of business if it were not for the profit from their charge accounts.

Think about this. If your charge account goes

over 30 days, in some cases 90 days, the store where you made the purchases is actually *lending* you the money for the unpaid balance—with interest. And money lending is big business!

The "Truth-in-Lending Act," passed by the United States Congress in 1969, took the cloak of secrecy off the mysterious "finance charge." The lender, or charge account seller, must give you the actual annual percentage rate of interest, as well as the dollar amount of interest charged.

Take a look at the small print somewhere on your charge account statement. You will probably see something like this: "Monthly interest rate 1½ per cent." This varies in different states, but it doesn't sound like much, does it? Read on.

The annual percentage rate will be listed as 18 per cent. Compare this to other annual percentage rates in the lending market. An automobile loan may be as high as 12 per cent; a home mortgage loan, depending on the going rate, anywhere from 7 to 10 per cent. Will you agree that to pay an annual percentage rate of 18 per cent on day-to-day purchases is not good money management?

If you were to ask, "Are you for, or against, credit cards?" I would have to reply, "It all depends."

Let's sum it up.

- Credit cards are convenient.
- Credit cards are safer than cash.
- They do NOT extend your income.
- They are NOT another kind of money.
- They can be properly used,
  or badly abused.

I am for credit cards when they are used within the limits of your monthly budget. I am against them when they become a reckless way of buying yourself into debt.

I have to admit that when Mike and Lynn are out of debt, and once again take possession of their charge cards, I will be praying that they will have learned their lesson. It will all depend on whether, or not, they learn to say, "We can't afford it."

CHAPTER SIX

Learning to Say, "I Can't Afford It"

What a difference a date makes—especially when it is with your wife. With his head in the air, and a spring in his step, Mike bounded up my walk. As he handed me his coat, I noticed that this time his eyes were smiling.

As we automatically headed for the dining room, he said, "I took Lynn out for dinner last night—and we talked. We talked more than we have in months."

"I'm so glad, Mike," I said. "Tell me about it."

"Well, for one thing, we know that we want to get back together," he said with determination.

Then, he went on to explain.

"We both agreed, however, that we need some

time to find out where we went wrong. We don't want to repeat the same mistakes."

I nodded my approval.

Rearranging his lanky frame in the chair, he added, "Lynn has already started counseling with the pastor. He wants her to come once a week, and as soon as he is ready I am going with her."

More than Mike's finances were on the road to recovery. A new, improved future for him and Lynn was beginning to take shape. It was the answer to many prayers.

Before we tackled the budget for this payday, Mike brought me up-to-date. Lynn had agreed to give up the apartment and the move was scheduled for Monday night. Mike's grandmother was going to store their furniture. Lynn and Bobby were going to stay with her parents, and Mike would continue living with his.

Mike opened the bright red budget book, laid his checkbook on the table and unzipped his pocket calculator. Then, as if he couldn't put it off any longer, he blurted out, "I overspent a little on that dinner last night."

"How much is a little?" I asked.

"Well—we didn't realize when we ordered that everything on the menu was a la carte, and when the check came, it was over $25."

He made a real effort to make $25 sound like a "little."

The budget allowed Mike $20 spending money every two weeks. This had to cover his personal needs and an occasional day on the town with little Bobby. Spending $25 for one dinner meant that he had to "rob Peter to pay Paul." This was the moment I had dreaded in this financial togetherness.

"You knew before you went that it was an expensive restaurant, didn't you?" I asked.

"Yes, but that was where Lynn wanted to go." He was defending himself. "And, it was worth every penny of it."

I wanted to say, "Of course, it was worth it. Take her to the moon, if you can recapture what you have lost in your marriage."

But, this was not the answer.

Another of Mike's basic problems was about to come to the surface. It is the one that lurks behind practically every shattered budget. At sometime, we are all guilty of it. It is the inability to say to ourselves, or anyone else, "I can't afford it."

Lynn was fully aware of their shortage of money. She had had a hand in creating the problem. She should have said, "Can we afford it?" And, Mike should have felt free to reply, "No, we can't."

When you want to do something, or buy something, which you know you cannot afford, there are two ways in which you can react. You will find them both mentioned in Hebrews 13:5.

"Let your manner of life be without covetousness, and be content with such things as ye have . . ."

The first part of this verse warns against living a life that is controlled by a desire for things. We usually think of covetousness as wanting something that belongs to another person, but it also covers the unrestrained desire for things you cannot afford. This way of life is filled with discontent and—indebtedness.

Jesus said in Mark 7:21-22, "For from within, out of the heart of men, proceed evil thoughts, adulteries, fornications, murders, thefts, covetousness, wickedness, deceit, lasciviousness, an evil eye, blasphemy, pride, foolishness." The sin of covetousness is listed right along with those we like to think of as the "big" sins.

The second part of the verse, "and be content with such things as ye have," could well be engraved on the front of your budget book. This doesn't mean that you are not to set goals for the things in life that you want. It simply means to be happy and at peace with yourself as you live within *your* income.

In Philippians 4:4-7, Paul says, "Rejoice in the Lord always; and again I say rejoice. Let your moderation be known unto all men. The Lord is at hand. Be anxious for nothing, but in everything, by prayer and supplication with thanksgiving, let your requests be made known unto God. And the peace of God, which passeth all understanding, shall keep your hearts and minds through Christ Jesus."

In verse 11, in the same chapter, Paul states, " . . . I have learned, in whatever state I am, in this to be content." Even Paul had to *learn* to be content. And, if he could, in the face of all of his troubles, you can, too!

I like the last part of verse 5. "The Lord is at hand." You don't have to learn this lesson alone. Bring your requests to Him. He will teach you contentment—and give you peace as a bonus.

Mike admitted that he had never been able to say, "I can't afford it." The result: seven past-due charge accounts. These four little words are as important to good money management as facing reality, building a payment schedule, or moving into a bright red budget book.

Mike began paying bills, checking off each item as he went. Since there was no rent to pay this month, he had planned to have the extra $120 to apply on the charge accounts and doctor bills. His $25 dinner had caught up with him. Now, there was only $95.

Lovable, impulsive, unpredictable and full of surprises—that's Mike. Tonight was no exception. We were about to discuss how to best use the $95, when he said, "Oh, by the way, here are a couple of bills that came this week."

The return addresses on the envelopes quickly identified them as—book clubs!

I questioned Mike and learned that the books—and their bills—would keep coming on schedule until he canceled them. Then, he broke the news that he belonged, not to two, but four, book clubs!

"How did you ever get involved with four of these deals?" I asked.

"I don't really know," he answered, "I guess the offer always seemed too good to pass up."

This was a classic example of not saying, "I can't afford it." The timing was perfect.

If you are tempted to feel a bit smug and think, "I would never get mixed up with *four* book clubs," stop and think about it for a minute. If you have mismanaged your finances, look for your "bookclub." One young mother admitted that hers was falling for every "special" on baby photographs.

Mike agreed to cancel the book clubs. We paid the two bills and had $85 left to work with.

When extra money appears in the budget, deciding where to use it is important. Here's what to look for: the balance due and the size of the monthly payment. In Mike's budget,

BankAmericard had the largest balance, but the monthly payments were only $37. Department Store #1 was the second largest balance and the monthly payment required was $50. Since this would free the most dollars per month, we decided to add the $85 to the regular $50 payment in the budget. Mike turned to the "Record of Progress," and deducted the $135 payment from the balance due. This would be the first one to be eliminated.

As Mike closed the budget book, we both felt the strain of the evening.

"How about going over to the Ice Cream Shoppe and getting something just loaded with calories?" I asked.

Mike grinned, and with a twinkle in his eye, replied, "I'd really like to, but I can't afford it."

"For a lesson well-learned—I'll treat!" I gladly responded—and off we went.

CHAPTER SEVEN

Just Between Us Girls and That Friendly Supermarket

Over our hot fudge sundaes, piled high with whipped cream, Mike and I decided it was about time to include Lynn in our Friday night bill-sessions. Mike had a head start in learning how to manage their finances. She needed to catch up.

Lynn and I had had no contact since she and Mike had separated. I wasn't sure how she felt about my involvement in their personal finances, but if there was going to be any strain, I wanted it out of the way before our next meeting.

Early the next week, I picked up the phone, breathed a prayer and dialed the number.

"Hello, Lynn? Could you have lunch with me tomorrow?"

"I'd love to." She sounded pleased.

We met the next day at a lovely Mexican cafe in a nearby shopping center.

As the gaily uniformed waitress walked away with our order, we smiled at each other. It was good to see Lynn again. After a few minutes of the usual kind of chit-chat, Lynn opened the subject of finances.

"I appreciate what you are doing to help Mike get on top of his bills."

"*His* bills, Lynn?"

She winced. "I'm sorry," she said. "I guess they are *our* bills, aren't they?"

"That's right, Lynn," I gently replied. "I don't think either one of you could have gotten this deeply in debt all alone."

She nodded her agreement. This was the opening I needed.

"Do you understand the working arrangement Mike and I have regarding your finances?"

"I'm not sure," she replied.

"Let me explain. We have agreed to meet on the Friday before every payday. After all the bills have been paid for that part of the budget, no other check is to be written until we have first discussed it. If you were not one hundred per cent in agreement with this, it could create some problems.

"What kind of problems?" She had a puzzled look on her face.

"For openers, you might begin to feel that how you and Mike spend your money is none of my business."

"Mike doesn't seem to resent it," she said. "In fact, he's really excited about having a budget."

"I know," I smiled. "But, are you willing for the

same kind of togetherness, the same control? Mike wants you to come with him a week from this Friday. Instead of the usual two-peas-in-the-pod, there would be three."

Lynn laughed and said, "Count me in as pea number three."

As quickly as the laugh came, it disappeared. Fighting to keep the tears back, she quietly said, "I just know we need all the help we can get."

Now our team was complete. All members were present, accounted for—and ready to go. A sure guarantee for success.

We spent the next few minutes catching up on the problems to date in their financial mismanagement. They boiled down to these three: (1) Charging faster than they could pay. They were both impulsive spenders. (2) Trying to handle their finances without a schedule—no flight plan. Also known as "flying blind." (3) Not being able to say, "We can't afford it." A shortage of self-discipline.

Lynn was soaking it up like a blotter. She would be able to help Mike in so many areas.

"Mike is going to work on that third problem this week, Lynn, and he is going to need your encouragement and full cooperation."

"Oh, I'll really try," she promised.

Changing the subject somewhat, I said, "Just between us girls, where do you think you need the most help in managing money?"

She groaned. "I guess my biggest problem was running out of grocery money before payday!"

Can you sympathize with Lynn? I can, but let's face it. Those tempting, tantalizing items and displays at your friendly supermarket are out to get you! You have to enter the store with your guard

CHAPTER EIGHT

Aiming at Goals, One, Two and Three

The wind was whistling around the front door as I hurried to open it for Mike and Lynn. Hand-in-hand, they dashed into the house. They were both laughing. Shutting the door behind them, Mike breathlessly said, "Look what the wind blew in."

Taking her coat, I said, "Welcome, Lynn, we're glad to have you join us in the battle of the budget."

We headed for the dining room. Once again, Mike and I were on opposite sides of the table, but this time Lynn was close beside him. She seemed a little nervous.

Mike put his hand over hers on the table and said, "I know *I'm* happy she's here!"

That did it. She smiled at him, and then sitting up

straight, she looked at me as if to say, "Let's get started."

"Before we plunge into paying bills," I said, "there is something we need to discuss, O.K.?"

In unison, they said, "O.K."

This was probably the first time they had ever sat down together to discuss their finances and pay bills. Starting right was so important. Either one of them could defeat this effort. They had to realize the importance of working together, as a team—with each one lending the other strength when the temptation came to buy what they couldn't afford.

"Lynn," I began, "Mike has been making real progress whacking away at the mountain of bills you both managed to pile up. When you move into a new apartment, the budget will be even tighter. It is going to take every ounce of self-discipline you both can muster to hold the line until the last one is paid."

Lynn moved a little closer to Mike and slipped her arm through his.

"I don't want to sound like a prophet of doom," I continued, "but if you do not learn to manage your personal finances efficiently, the two of you don't have a ghost of a chance of making your marriage work. You won't last one year!"

A very sober Mike said, "I believe it."

It takes two to succeed. You cannot do it alone. If, while you are trying to gain control of runaway debts, your mate continues to charge and spend beyond your ability to pay—it just won't work. If the desire to balance your budget is one-sided, try to resolve it through an open, frank discussion. If this doesn't work, seek help and counsel from someone outside. A happy marriage depends on it.

Not realizing that I was touching a nerve, I added, "You need to agree right from the beginning that, if necessary, you will be each other's conscience. If one wants to buy something that you cannot afford, the other will have to remind the erring partner. And—that person must agree not to get mad when reminded!"

Lynn picked it right up. "It's like the other day, Mike wanted to buy something and I told him we couldn't afford it." She hesitated and then went on, "Are you saying that he should accept the reminder and not get mad at me?"

Mike blushed and sheepishly grinned at me.

"Mike, you didn't!"

"I'm afraid I did," he confessed.

Lynn hastened to defend him. "If the roles had been reversed, I probably would have reacted the same way. We'll both have to work at it."

Satisfied that they understood the consequences of not learning to manage their money with complete cooperation, I moved our attention to the bright red budget book.

Mike proudly started at the beginning and showed Lynn how each section worked—from the "Yearly Expenses," right on through to the "Record of Progress." She eagerly took it all in and then asked, "When can we start paying bills?"

Laughing at her impatience, I said, "How about right now?"

For the next half-hour, or so, they were lost in their world of "high finance." The characters! They were actually having fun paying bills.

When they finished, we decided to total the balances due on the seven charge accounts and see how much progress had been made. Picking up his little calculator, Mike started adding as Lynn read the balances out loud. We were amazed. The total due had been cut by a little over $500—in six short weeks! This led to the next subject on my list.

Goals!

Goals are the magic stimuli, or incentives, in life which incite you to do the impossible. A person without a goal ambles nonchalantly through life—accomplishing little. But, find the people who are making things happen and you will find goal-setters.

The Apostle Paul was no exception. In Philippians 3:13,14 we find his life goal. It's a good one for Mike and Lynn, and you, to follow.

" . . . this one thing I do, forgetting those things which are behind, and reaching forth unto those things which are before, I press toward the mark for the prize of the high calling of God in Christ Jesus."

Paul was not dealing with our particular subject of finances, but there is an excellent principle here. Forgetting the past—a way of life displeasing to God. And, reaching forth to the future and a life lived in the center of God's will. This is a spiritual goal and under its umbrella should come all of the physical and material goals in a Christian's life.

With this in mind, we are going to look at three very down-to-earth, practical goals. They are the *immediate,* the *short-term* and the *long-range.* It is important to work these out together. When you have them clearly defined, list them in the front of your book as a reminder to *reach* for them.

There was no question about this young couple's *immediate goal.* It was to reunite their family. This would require one month's rent and the security, or damage, deposit on a new apartment.

We turned to the "Payday/Budget Date Schedule" in the front of their budget book to see how soon it could help them reach that goal.

Sure enough! There was one of those free and clear paychecks coming up. It wasn't going to be as soon as they had hoped, but we earmarked it for that purpose.

Without too much discussion, they agreed that their *short-term goal* was two-pronged. The elimination of those seven charge accounts—and the installation of the full tithe. To reach this goal and have it qualify as "short-term," would demand consistent payments every payday and patient adherence to the "no charge policy."

A *long-range goal* seems harder to reach, simply because it takes longer. But, it is the kind that makes a dream come true. Your dream may be to take a trip around the world, own your own home, acquire more education, start your own business—or perhaps own a 40-foot yacht. Whatever it is, it will never happen unless you *start* reaching for it.

Inspired by all of this goal setting, Mike said, "I know that before too long we want our own home."

There it was.

All three goals were clearly defined. Mike and Lynn could see how they were going to manage the first two, but the third was going to be a bit more difficult—or so they thought.

I had been waiting to introduce Mike and Lynn to a more positive side of personal finances. The automatic savings account. This was an ideal time.

"As soon as you have reached your short-term goals, I would like to get you started with two automatic savings accounts," I announced.

CHAPTER NINE

The Unseen Dollars Behind Your Dream House

Mike had been talking with one of the young men at work who was getting ready to buy a $30,000 house with a VA loan—and no down payment. Mike was excited at the prospect and their long-range goal seemed to move closer—right up to the end of those seven charge accounts.

As we discussed this one evening, I asked, "Do you have any idea, Mike, what it costs to move into a new house?"

Mike was only looking at the $30,000 and that isn't even the beginning. There are some unseen dollars behind Mike's dream house that need to be considered. I decided to get some facts and figures and when the time comes, help Mike and Lynn go into home ownership with their eyes open, aware of the different options and with the tools to make wise decisions.

There is a fine Christian real estate agent in Denver named, Haskal Gallimore. I shared with him my concern for young couples who jump into buying a "dream house" only to find out a few months later that it has turned into a nightmare. And all because they were not aware of the total expenses involved in buying—and owning a house.

Haskal agreed to help and then said, "In dealing with young couples, I try to find out if they can afford to buy the house in question. If I know they are getting in too deep, I advise against it."

There no doubt are others who feel the same way, but unfortunately, too many real estate salesmen, and saleswomen, are only interested in making the sale. And too many people, of all ages, get caught up in the excitement of buying a new house and fail to raise the questions that I hope we will put into your mind.

We decided to use specific examples to illustrate the choices that may be open to you when buying a house. For the first example, let's take a *new* house selling for $30,000. And since Mike and Lynn would probably elect to go with a VA loan, we will, too. The same formula, however, can be used to analyze any mortgage proposal.

We'll assume it is a full (no down payment) VA loan, at 7¾ per cent interest per annum and that they plan to amortize it over 30 years. One of the first questions you need to have answered is, "Can we afford the monthly payment?"

Four items need to be taken into account in arriving at the figure that will have to appear in your budget in place of rent. They are: principal, interest, taxes and insurance. The first two are referred to as "P & I," and all four as, "P.I.T.I."

Here is the monthly payment breakdown on our first example:

```
Principal and interest ......... $214.93
Taxes (approximate) .........    44.00
Insurance ...................     9.00
        Total P.I.T.I. ........... $267.93
```

To qualify for this loan, Mike and Lynn will need *four* times this amount, or $1,072 gross income per month. That is, *if* they have no other payments, except for utilities. When the seven charge accounts and the car are paid off, they *could* move in. It would, however, be a foolish thing to do, for it isn't really that simple.

Most new houses come equipped with carpets, a stove, hood with fan, garbage disposal and dishwasher. You will have to provide the washer, dryer, refrigerator, drapes and landscaping. In that number two savings account, you should have enough money to cover the following:

```
Closing costs ...................$  500
Appliances .....................   675
Drapes (minimum) .............  1,000
Landscaping (minimum) ........  1,200
        Total ...............$3,375
```

If you were going to finalize this deal as listed, you would need at least $4,000 set aside to pay for the beginning expenses. (The additional $625 would help cover the unanticipated extras that accompany a move into a new house.) If you were to sign on the dotted line—and didn't have it—can you picture the charges and installment payments that would once again appear in your budget?

Once you have decided to buy a house, don't rush into it. Wait until you have saved the money needed to do it right. And then, ask questions and get answers! Few lending agencies will *offer* this information. Here are a few choices open to you:

You can . . .
- buy a new house, or an older one;
- apply for a VA (for veterans), an FHA or a conventional loan;
- choose to amortize it over 30 years, 25 years, or less;
- make no down payment on some loans;
- pay 10 or 20 per cent down on others;
- assume an existing loan.

When assuming an existing loan, investigate the interest rate. It can be raised to meet the going rate. The interest, however, does not escalate on an existing VA loan.

Let's see how your decision can affect your investment dollar. Since taxes and insurance remain the same, we'll work only with the P & I payment. Here's how to find out the interest you will pay on a full VA, 30 year loan:

$$\$214.93 \times 360 \text{ months} = \$77,374.80$$

$$\begin{array}{r} \text{Less price of house} \quad \underline{30,000.00} \\ \text{Interest paid} \quad \overline{\$47,374.80} \end{array}$$

That's a bit of a shock, even if you were expecting it!

Now, see what happens if you elect to make a down payment. With a VA loan this is called a "privilege." For every $1,000 you pay down, you can deduct from $7 to $17 from your monthly P & I payment.

We'll average it out to $14 for ease in figuring and assume that you have $3,000, or 10 per cent, to pay down. That would take $42 off of the $214.93 and bring the P & I payment down to $172.93. Follow this through:

$$
\begin{array}{rr}
\$172.93 \times 360 \text{ months} = & \$62,254.80 \\
\text{Add down payment} & 3,000.00 \\
\hline
\text{Total paid} & \$65,254.80 \\
\text{Less price of house} & 30,000.00 \\
\hline
\text{Interest paid} & \$35,254.80 \\
\end{array}
$$

Without the down payment the interest paid was, $47,374.80. You have just saved $12,120.00 as a result of the $3,000 down payment. But your financial expertise doesn't end there. Don't forget the $42 per month you have saved on the P & I payment. If you hadn't made the down payment, it would have had to be paid every month. And, *if* you were to put it in the bank, here's what it would amount to—not even counting interest earned.

$$
\begin{array}{rr}
\$42 \times 360 \text{ months} = & \$15,120.00 \\
\text{Plus interest saved} & 12,120.00 \\
\hline
\text{Total gained} & \$27,240.00 \\
\end{array}
$$

And all because of the automatic savings account!

Now, let's see what happens if you decide to shorten the amortization period from 30 to 25 years, or 300 months. It will *add* $11.67 to your monthly P & I payment, bringing it up to $226.60. Add the taxes and insurance and your monthly P.I.T.I. payment would be $279.60. Your gross monthly income would have to be $1,118.

$226.60 × 300 months =	$67,980.00
Less price of house	30,000.00
Interest paid	$37,980.00

A savings of $9,394.80! And all you had to invest was the additional $11.67 per month, or a total of $3,501. (This is without a down payment.)

For our second illustration, we decided to investigate a ten year old house, selling for the same price—$30,000. For an equal comparison, it will also be a full VA, 30 year loan. On an older house, the interest rate jumps to 8½ per cent per annum. The closing costs, taxes and insurance are the same. Due to the higher interest rate, the monthly P & I payment will be $230.68. Add the taxes and insurance and your *monthly payment* would be $283.68. To qualify for this loan you would have to have a gross income of $1,134.72 per month, with no other payments, except utilities.

There are some advantages in considering an older house. It usually includes everything you find in a new house, plus the drapes, refrigerator and fully developed landscaping. (You can often negotiate for the washer and dryer.) Here is the cash you would need:

Closing costs..............	$500
Washer and dryer..........	375
Total..............	$875

There are also some disadvantages to consider if

you decide to buy an older house. You may be "inheriting" ten year old appliances, hot water heater and furnace. The carpet and drapes may be ready for replacement. You may find yourself strapped with expensive repairs within a few months. Check these out before signing any papers.

Now, let's follow this P & I payment through to a conclusion:

$230.68 × 360 months = $83,044.80
Less price of house   30,000.00
Interest paid $53,044.80

For every $1,000 paid down, you can deduct $7.69 from the monthly P & I payment. If you pay $3,000 down and deduct $23.07, you will bring the P & I payment down to $207.61. (Don't forget to add taxes and insurance.)

$207.61 × 360 months = $74,739.60
Add down payment   3,000.00
Total paid $77,739.60
Less price of house   30,000.00
Interest paid $47,739.60

Without the down payment, the interest was $53,044.80. A savings of $5,305.20.

If you shorten the length of the loan to 25 years and add the $11.67 to the $230.68 P & I payment, it will look like this:

$242.35 × 300 months = $72,705.00
Less price of house   30,000.00
Interest paid $42,705.00

Before you get discouraged with all of these interest figures, there is something else you need to consider. If you were to continue renting an apartment, or house, at an average cost of $250 per month, here is what it would come to for 25 and 30 years:

$$\$250 \times 300 \text{ months} = \$75,000$$
$$\$250 \times 360 \text{ months} = \$90,000$$

The monthly payment in the first example given was, $267.93 for 30 years.

$$\$267.93 \times 360 \text{ months} = \$96,454.80$$
$$\text{Less rent for same} \quad \underline{\quad 90,000.00}$$
$$\text{Difference} \quad \overline{\$\ 6,454.80}$$

If you continue to rent, all you will have to show for that $90,000 is a very large pile of rent receipts. When you buy a house, however, you are investing your dollars and building your fixed assets. And, the interest and taxes—every dollar paid—can be deducted yearly from your income tax report.

Buying a house is a good investment—as soon as you are ready to take on the payments and the responsibility. All I want you to do is investigate all of the possibilities before signing a contract. As long as we have inflation, the house you buy this year will be worth more next year!

I'm not even going to tell you what kind of a house, or loan, you should consider. This chapter is to stimulate your thinking and help you see the need to research the facts and make the wisest decision—for you.

I want Mike and Lynn to have their dream house,

but not before they are ready. If they go into it without the cash necessary to make the monthly payments fit comfortably into the budget, they will soon feel trapped with the responsibility of owning a house.

If, however, they carefully plan and stay in control of their finances, they will *enjoy* the privileges and problems of being home owners.

Don't ignore the unseen dollars behind *your* dream house!

CHAPTER TEN

Looking For Alternatives Can Be Fun

There is more than one way to "skin a cat"—or to do almost anything in life. And, Mike and Lynn were busy discovering this. Their youthful ingenuity and imagination were hard at work. They were looking for "another way" of getting the money to tie down that new apartment—without waiting for the "due process" of the bright red budget book!

Too excited to wait for our regular Friday meeting, Mike called me at home one evening.

"Hi!" his voice boomed over the telephone. "Guess what?"

Almost afraid to find out, I said, "I can't imagine, Mike. Tell me."

"You know that watch I bought in Germany?

Well, I sold it!"

"That's great, Mike. What did you do with the money?" I hastened to ask.

"Oh, we put it in the bank," he said. "But that isn't all."

"You mean there's more?"

"Yes," he rushed on, "Remember that old hide-a-bed we had in our other apartment? We sold that, too."

Before I could slip a word in edgewise, he added, "And, a fellow at work is going to buy our old black and white TV set. He's going to give me the money payday."

Silence.

He had either run out of breath—or old items to sell.

"Mike, I'm proud of you! What made you think of selling those things?" I asked.

Then, he explained what I had already guessed.

"We're anxious to decide on an apartment and we thought that if we could come up with the deposit and the rent before payday, we could have it all ready to move into by the first of the month. And—the rent money that's already in the budget can be used to pay bills."

"Good thinking, Mike," I said.

"We have found one we like," he added. "Will you go with us to look at it?"

We did look at the apartment. It was lovely; two bedrooms, gold carpeting and gold appliances. They chose one on the garden level. It was considerably less expensive than the first and second floor apartments. And, best of all it fit into the budget. Mike proudly paid the deposit. They could move in in two weeks.

The fulfillment of their first—and immediate—goal was just around the corner. They were on cloud nine.

Perhaps you are thinking, "But, we don't have any old furniture, or antique watches to sell." It really doesn't matter. Raising money through a "second-hand business" is not the moral to this story. But, this is. Looking for alternatives can be the difference between being miserable and having fun during your financial crunch.

Oh, you can force yourself to "endure to the end," indulging in self-pity every inch of the way. But, I hope you won't. The idea of looking for "another way" of doing things can be applied to almost anything. It adds a spark of adventure and fun to life—while you are learning to say, "We can't afford it."

If what you want to buy—or do—is too expensive for your budget, look for the alternative. Be careful, however, that the "other way" isn't also too costly. There are times when the alternate is just doing without.

Think about this. People who are miserable are usually unhappy with themselves. If you are keeping pace with Mike and Lynn, the worry and frustration of unpaid debts have been replaced with a planned recovery. You are now in control of your battered finances. Not out of debt, but in control. This should make you feel good about yourself.

And, while you are teaching yourself all of these character-building lessons, you can stop taking life and "things" for granted, and start having the time of your life discovering the simple joys in the world around you.

One day at lunch, Mike was telling me about a

book he was reading. It included ideas on ways husbands could keep their wives happy.

"There was one great idea," he related, "and when I can afford it, I'm going to do it for Lynn. You make a coupon book and write things on each one that you think your wife would like."

Intrigued, I asked, "What kind of things?"

"Well, for example, it suggested one coupon that would read, 'Good for $25 and a day free to go shopping. Baby-sitting provided.' Another was to be, 'Good for one dinner date with your husband at your favorite restaurant.' "

"That sounds like fun, but why wait until you can afford it?" I asked.

"What do you mean?" Mike was interested.

"It's part of a game called 'looking for the alternative,' " I replied.

"Go on. I'm listening." Mike was beginning to see the light.

"All right, Mike. How about this? 'Good for one breakfast in bed on the day of your choice.' Or, 'Good for one deluxe shampoo.' Or, 'Good for one large pizza on a night when you least feel like cooking.' "

"Wow! I see what you mean. I can use the same idea, but make out coupons that cost very little, or nothing in the way of money."

Mike had an opportunity to practice this principle the very next day. He and Lynn had stopped by my office to talk about the move into the new apartment.

"I'll have to get some new bookcases," Mike announced. He had discarded the old metal ones when they moved out of the other apartment.

Lynn looked horrified, and I quickly interjected, "Mike, you can't *afford* new bookcases."

He got the point and quickly agreed. All of the beautiful books that had been piling up from those four book clubs would just have to stay in their boxes for a little longer—or would they?

"Mike," I said, "is there another way of getting bookcases, without buying them?"

We all began to think.

Finally, Mike said, "We could make them."

"Yes, but out of what?" Lynn asked.

Turning to Mike, I asked, "Would cinder blocks work for the ends?" I had just remembered a few extras in my basement.

They took over from there!

Mike said, "My dad has some odd pieces of lumber in the garage."

Lynn added, "And my dad will let us use his electric sander."

Mike went to work. He cut the boards to size and gave them a thorough sanding. Then, with a can of white spray paint for the cinder blocks and a can of varnish for the shelves, he turned out a handsome set of book shelves for their new apartment—and all those books. The budget wasn't disturbed and the alternate idea more than satisfied the need.

This system—looking for alternatives—takes a little practice, but before long you will begin bumping into ideas everywhere you turn. How about the entertainment areas, or the leisure hours, in your life? Will it work there? Absolutely!

Here are a few ideas to start your wheels turning:

A walk, hand-in-hand, in the rain,
   the wind,
      the snow,
         the sunlight—or the moonlight.

A rousing game of tennis,
  Frisbe,
    Monopoly with friends,
      Checkers or chess for two, or, any other no-
cost game.
  A picnic in the park,
    the country, the beach,
      the mountains,
        the backyard—the frontyard,
          or on the living room floor.
How about a pot-luck dinner
  with another couple,
    your neighbors,
      someone who is lonely,
        or even your family?
Do you have bicycles? Ride them
  around the lake,
    the block,
      through the park,
or any other place bikes can go.

We haven't even mentioned sharing a good book, or seeing your hometown through the eyes of a tourist. I have actually lived in Denver all of my life and have never paid a visit to the mint!

Yes, you can have fun looking for alternatives, once you have developed the habit. And, when you have, you will discover that the most expensive way of doing—and buying—is not always the best, or the most fun!

Remember Paul? " . . . for I have learned, in whatever state I am, in this to be content."

Enjoy yourselves on the road to a balanced budget!

CHAPTER ELEVEN

A Sane Approach to Your Insurance Needs

"Are you going to include a chapter on the insurance needs of young couples?" A friend called me at the office one morning with this question.

"It doesn't happen to be one of Mike and Lynn's problems," I replied, "but I have been considering it."

She went on to tell me why she was so concerned. Her son and his young wife had just bought a life insurance policy with a $40 monthly premium.

"And they just can't afford it!" she said.

I decided to talk the problem over with a friend, Paul Riley, who has been in the insurance business for 28 years. Paul has a reputation of giving young couples an honest evaluation of their insurance needs in the light of their ability to pay—before recommending coverage. He had helped Mike and Lynn with their insurance needs.

As we talked, Paul agreed that many young people are no match for an aggressive, unprincipled insurance salesman. He explained, however, that the pressure to sell a product that is intangible is great. Especially on the young insurance salesman. He can't walk into your home and tempt you to purchase a shiny set of pots and pans, show you a beautiful set of books, or demonstrate a powerful new vacuum cleaner. He has to rely on his convincing sales pitch. He is selling protection and you can neither see, nor touch it.

And just like the friendly supermarket, he is out to sell you as much as possible, whether you can afford it or not. His job depends on it. *Your* assignment is to find an insurance man whom you can trust: one who has *your* best interest at heart and who will advise you wisely. There are many like this. Be sure you find one before deciding on an insurance program.

Whether you select your agent, or his company first, is not important. Both must measure up. There are about 2,000 insurance companies in the United States and Canada. And, of this number only about 800 can be considered wise choices.

The insurance company you do business with should be licensed in your state and have a good financial record. It should be a proven company—one with a good track record in paying claims.

If you have questions, or doubts, about a company, or agent, you can contact the Insurance

Department, or Board, in your state. They will give you an honest answer to your inquiry.

"There's no one with endurance,
Like the man who sells insurance."

I don't know where, or when, I first heard this little jingle, but it has had a strange effect on my reaction to this profession. When my secretary tells me that a "Mr. Smith with the XYZ Insurance company is on the line," my resistance immediately shifts into gear.

And yet, insurance is a product that we all need. Like anything else you buy, however, it must meet your particular needs—and also fit into *your* budget.

There are four kinds of insurance that you will want to consider. They are:

> Medical Insurance
> Automobile Insurance
> Home Owner's Insurance
> Life Insurance

With the inflationary spiral of hospital and medical expenses today, it is important to be covered with a good *medical insurance* policy.

Mike and Lynn have Blue Cross/Blue Shield coverage under the group plan where he works. The amount is automatically deducted from his salary once a month. (We didn't even list it in their budget.)

Due to complications when little Bobby was born, Mike and Lynn had over $6,000 in hospital and doctor bills in one year. Without medical insurance, it would have been a financial disaster. It will, however, be ten years before they will have paid that much in insurance payments.

If your employer has a group plan for health insurance, be sure you are enrolled. Group coverage is usually better and also less expensive than an individual policy. Don't put this off. Youth is no guarantee against accident or illness. And, even a brief stay in the hospital can cost thousands of dollars.

Automobile insurance is probably the first kind of insurance you were introduced to—on the day you started driving your own car. Banks and lending agencies require this coverage while you are paying for your car. In many states the law requires liability insurance. It is wise to buy from a well-established, reputable firm.

The rates are usually determined by your age, your driving record, the kind of car you drive, and the coverage you desire. You may have your choice of paying once, or twice, a year. The two payment plan is easier to fit into a tight budget.

Home owner's insurance is required by the bank holding the mortgage on your house. It protects you—and the bank—against loss by fire, lightning, theft, vandalism, etc. This is a part of your P.I.T.I. monthly house payment.

If you are renting an apartment or house, you may want to consider "household content" insurance. The only difference between this and the home owner's policy is that it does not cover the dwelling. For this reason it is much less expensive.

Life insurance is a more complex package, partly because there are so many different plans and combinations offered. I won't even attempt to present individual insurance programs and policies. Yours should be tailor-made for you and your family. There are some things, in a general way, that may help you ask the right questions and be prepared to judge the value of various insurance proposals.

It isn't necessarily true that life insurance should be purchased when you are young just to save on the premium rates. The rates do not actually change that much—until you reach the age of 40. This myth often leads young couples into buying a policy that is much too large for their needs, and their ability to pay the monthly premium.

Life insurance is an enigma. It is the only thing in the world that will pay its face value after only one payment and in some cases before *any* payment has been made. A person can take out a $10,000 life insurance policy, die the next week and his family will receive the entire face value of $10,000.

On the other hand, if you take out more insurance than you can afford and have to drop it before it matures, you will take a big loss on your investment. Here is an approximate schedule of the loss you would take by cashing your policy in at 2, 5 and 10 years:

$$2 \text{ years } \ldots \ldots \ldots 90 \text{ per cent loss}$$
$$5 \text{ years } \ldots \ldots \ldots 60 \text{ per cent loss}$$
$$10 \text{ years } \ldots \ldots \ldots 25 \text{ per cent loss}$$

By the 15th anniversary you would begin to show a gain. It is far better to start with a policy that you can afford and keep it until maturity. Remember, you can always add additional insurance as your income increases in future years.

There are basically two types of life insurance offered. We'll just touch on these. They are *permanent* life insurance and *term* life insurance.

There are three popular permanent life insurance plans. They guarantee the age at date of issue and create cash and loan values for future years. The premiums remain the same for the life of the policy.

Plan One: Whole, or Straight, Life Insurance

> The premiums continue on this plan as long as the insured lives. It can be cashed in at any time. The premiums are usually lower than the other plans.

Plan Two: Limited Life Plan

> This policy is *paid up* in a specific number of years. The premiums stop at this point and the face value of the policy is held by the insurance company as a death benefit.

Plan Three: Endowment Plan

> The difference between this plan and the Limited Life Plan is that when it matures, the face value is paid to the insured and the policy canceled.

Term insurance is something worth considering. The premiums are low and it is a good way of getting started with an insurance program. One real advantage is that it can later be converted to a permanent plan—and the insurance company guarantees the best rate at the time of conversion.

Also, term insurance premiums are at an all time low for initial premiums. Large term policies, such as a 5 year renewable policy, are in may cases 50 per cent lower now than they were in 1959. You can buy this type of insurance for about $3 per year per $1,000 of life insurance protection. A $25,000 policy would run about $75 a year.

Some salesmen don't push term insurance because their commission is based on the low premium, rather than on the amount of the policy as it is on a permanent plan.

Here are three plans under term insurance:

Plan One: Group Term Life Insurance

Many businesses offer this group coverage for their employees. The rates are low and the policy is in effect as long as the individual is employed by the company. No physical qualification is required.

Plan Two: Level Term Insurance

This policy is taken out by an individual for a specific period of time. The face value and the premium remain the same. It may be renewed, or converted to a permanent plan. The premium will increase, however, to agree with the rate for the current age of the insured. Some type of physical qualification is required.

Plan Three: Reducing Term Insurance

This is much the same as the Level Term plan, except the face value decreases and the premium remains the same.

There is also a term rider which can be added to a permanent policy. You may wish to start with a small amount of permanent, low premium insurance with a sizeable term rider. Later when your income is larger and you are established in your career, you can convert the term insurance to a larger permanent plan.

My concern, however, is not what kind of insurance you purchase. Helping you to ask the right questions and be aware of the various options open to you, is the purpose of this chapter.

Here are a few things you should *not* buy from an insurance salesman—if you are a young couple, or young single person.

> *Estate Planning:* If you are young it is too early and premature to assume there is an estate and when you haven't had time to create perhaps anything but debts.

> *A Retirement Plan:* This is also premature since careers are not yet established and cash will be needed to start your savings program and pay off obligations for things needed to settle your home.

> *Insurance on a Financed Plan:* In other words, do not sign a promissory note to pay insurance premiums. Most State Insurance Departments allow this and many small companies encourage this practice. It is dangerous. There is little, or no cash value in the early years of a life insurance policy and you stand to lose nearly all of your investment when you are forced to pay the note, plus the interest.

Here are a few pointers to help you spot a trustworthy insurance salesman:

1. If he starts by reviewing your present insurance policies and other fringe benefits you already have, it is the first sign that he is interested in *you.*

2. If he is willing to show you the rates and plans from his rate book for your last age so you can

compare them with the package he is presenting, you know he is being fair.

3. If he shows you several combinations in a simple way from his rate book it is a real indication that he is trying to help you.

I'm glad that Mike and Lynn found the right insurance man in the beginning years of their marriage. And, I hope you have, too. But, if you are in too deep already, set out to get the right advice and correct the situation before you have invested too much in a program you can't handle.

CHAPTER TWELVE

The Joy
of a Bill Marked
"Paid"

Another Friday evening, only this time I was standing outside the door of Mike and Lynn's new apartment. They had invited me to dinner—and tomorrow was payday.

Three short months had slipped by, almost unnoticed, since Mike and I had had our first meeting. It didn't seem possible! So much had happened. They had completed their counseling with the pastor; they were back together as a family—and they were in control of their personal finances.

With my finger on the doorbell, I hesitated just a moment to say, "Thank you, Lord, for everything!"

I pushed the doorbell. The door opened and there stood Mike and Lynn—looking so *right*. And, from his room came little Bobby on the run, grinning from ear to ear. Once again, everything was all right in his world.

I was barely inside when Mike asked, "Shall we eat first, or pay bills?"

Mike would rather eat than almost anything, so I knew something in that budget book had him excited. Then, I remembered. The extra money from the rent was burning a hole in his checkbook!

I glanced at Lynn's beautiful table. The candles were already lit.

"Let's eat first," I said. "The budget will wait."

It was a happy dinner—and Lynn's individual meat loaves were just perfect. She gave me a knowing smile as she served Mike his.

Almost as fast as Lynn and I had cleared the table, Mike arrived from the other room with the checkbook, the budget book and his trusty little calculator. This time we were around *their* table.

"What shall we do with the extra money?" Mike began.

"Why don't we pay our regular bills first, Mike?" Lynn suggested. "And when we know how much is left, we can decide the best place to put it, O.K.?"

Mike laughed.

"Sure," he said. "That makes sense. I'm just so anxious to see what we can accomplish with it."

He handed Lynn the checkbook and she began writing the checks. As Mike made the entries and check marks in the budget book, he said, "You know, this bright red budget book is becoming a way of life."

"That's the idea," I replied.

The key to good money management is consistency. Once you have built your payment schedule, stick to it. Of course, you will need to adjust it as you review your priorities from time to time. Circumstances have a way of changing these.

Hopefully, before long, you will be paying off some of your bills. This will free those dollars to be used someplace else. Don't let them slip through your fingers! Decide immediately where you want to reschedule them.

This may be the time you will want to increase your giving; double up on another debt; open a savings account—or perhaps all three—depending on the amount you have to work with.

It was gratifying to see that Mike was thinking along these lines. He had their short-term goals clearly in focus.

When the last check mark was in place, Mike totaled the checks written and gave us the amount left. They both looked at me—waiting for me to suggest where to put the extra money. Instead of telling them where I thought it should go, I said, "Why don't you turn to your 'Record of Progress' section and take a look at all seven accounts. Then, you decide where the wisest payment could be made."

Mike had learned last month what to look for when he had the $85 left after that $25 dinner and the book club payments!

But would he remember?

Even little birds have to be pushed out of the nest if they are going to learn to fly—and it was about time to test Mike and Lynn's wings.

They began studying each account. Mike seemed to be thinking out loud, but Lynn was listening. This was her first exposure to this kind of decision.

"Hm-m-m, the largest balance is still on BankAmericard, but the monthly payment is only $37. If we pay it here, the balance will be lower, but we would still have the payment in the budget."

Then, he turned back to Department Store #1.

"On the other hand—this account has a fixed payment of $50 and . . ."

Now he was getting excited.

" . . . and—with the regular payment already in the budget—WE COULD WIPE IT OUT!"

He calmed down just a bit and explained to Lynn, "This would eliminate $50 from the payment schedule and free that much for . . ." He stopped.

I laughed and said, "Mike, you did it! That's exactly what I would have suggested."

Handing the checkbook to Lynn, he said, "Man, you have to think these things through, don't you?"

Lynn gleefully wrote out the check while Mike entered the extra payment on the record of progress for Department Store #1. This was their first "zero" balance. With a flourish he wrote, "Paid in Full," across the page—and signed his name.

"I think we should all autograph this page," he said, and handed the book to Lynn.

Laughing with excitement, Lynn added her name and handed the book across the table to me.

Oh, the joy of a bill marked, "Paid."

One down—and six to go.

In the beginning of this book, I admitted that it would not present a highly technical budget program. And, of course, it doesn't, but I hope you are catching the spirit of excitement, and yes, even fun, of gaining control of your unruly finances. Once you are out of debt, you may want to move on to a more detailed, sophisticated plan. And, that is fine. The important thing is to continue having a plan!

Don't run the risk of a repeat performance.

"Where shall we schedule the extra $50?" Lynn wanted to know.

"It won't appear in the budget again until next month," I said, "so why don't we wait until then to decide? By then you will know if we have allowed enough for your regular living expenses."

"It *was* hard to make the grocery money stretch," she admitted.

When Mike and Lynn moved into the new apartment, their living expenses increased overnight. The budget didn't allow room in which to even wiggle. They needed a bit more breathing space.

Even this wouldn't last long, for there was another large expense looming on the horizon. As much as we all, especially Mike, wished it would just go away, we knew it wouldn't. Sooner, or later, it would have to be faced.

Mike needed extensive dental work. It had already been postponed too long. Increasingly, Mike appeared with a swollen face from a tooth that was acting up. He hated to bring the subject out in the open.

"I have an appointment to see about my teeth next week. We may need it to make the payments on that bill."

Mike and Lynn were not going to be free from financial pressures for a long time, but together they were learning to handle them bravely—and with contentment.

The joy of that first bill marked, "Paid," was just the encouragement they needed!

CHAPTER THIRTEEN

Cutting The Budget Pie Into Pieces

The happy payday arrived when Mike and Lynn were able to pay off Department Store #2. I was delighted to hear Mike say, "Let's add $5 a payday to our tithe."

The balance of that payment would go toward the other charge accounts. The "Record of Progress" section in the budget book was the visual proof that Mike and Lynn were gaining on those seven charge accounts.

Anticipating a debt-free future, Lynn said, "We were reading an article the other day about setting up a budget on percentages. Would that give us the guidelines necessary to keep this from ever happening again?"

Let's find out.

If you have read many articles, or books, on the management of personal finances, you no doubt have run into this theory. The most popular breakdown seems to be the 10-20-70 percentage scale, or some list it as 10-70-20. Everyone seems to agree that the 70 per cent is for "living expenses," and the 10 per cent for "saving, or investing."

One writer said the 20 per cent was "yours to enjoy," while another designated it as a "debts and buffer fund." I have to admit that these figures sound great, but I also have to ask, "Are they practical?"

Will they work in today's inflationary economy?

In all the percentage charts I have seen, the 100 per cent is based on your income *after* Federal, State and Social Security taxes have been deducted. You are required by law to pay taxes. How much you pay is not your decision. The amount you receive in your check on payday, after taxes, is commonly called, "take-home pay." To keep this clear, we will refer to income *before* taxes as "gross income," and *after* taxes as "net income."

If the article, or book, on finances is written from a Christian point of view, the 100 per cent almost always begins after taxes *and* the tithe have been deducted. Let me hasten to say that I am not trying to debate the subject, but it does seem rather odd for a Christian to place the tithe in the same category with taxes. It makes the tithe an impersonal, automatic obligation with no place in your 100 per cent budget plan.

This brings to the surface the two schools of thought on how the tithe should be figured. Many Christians firmly believe that the tithe should be based on the gross income. Others feel it should be calculated on the net income—take-home pay. The decision, I believe, rests solely between the individual and the Lord.

In our chapter on tithing, we found that our giving should come from a willing mind and a heart of love. If your giving is motivated by fear, it becomes a legal obligation. If you are motivated by love, it is a spiritual blessing to give. When Christ is truly Lord of your life, you naturally will want to give all that you can. The New Testament, however, also teaches that you are to give out of what you have and not out of what you have not. Your giving has to be realistic.

We decided to take Mike and Lynn's income and apply the percentage system. We worked it up three ways just for fun! First, we took the total, gross income to see what per cent goes into taxes. They took the top 20 per cent of Mike's pay. We used the accepted 25 per cent for housing. This has to include the principal, interest, taxes and insurance (P.I.T.I.) in the payment. We added the 10 per cent based on gross income for the tithe.

Since insurance seldom appears as a separate listing in percentage plans, we took Mike and Lynn's actual insurance amounts. They were Blue Cross/Blue Shield, automobile insurance and a limited life insurance plan. This took a slice out of their budget pie of 8 per cent.

Next, we added the 10 per cent recommended for savings, or investments. This is where the *two* savings accounts would come from. Add these up and you will discover that we have exactly 27 per cent left to cover the following items:

Groceries
Car payment
Transportation
Clothing
Doctor bills
Medicine
Recreation
Miscellaneous

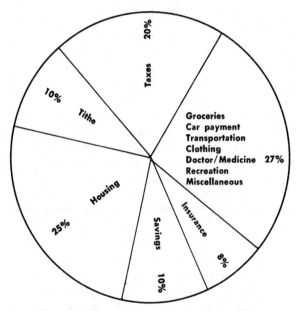

Total Gross Income

We had to abandon this pie in a hurry. There is no way that 27 per cent can cover the above expenses. The only item on the list that some might question is the car payment. But, let's be realistic. Most young couples *are* paying on a car. And, today in most areas a car is a necessity.

Next, we made an "after tax and tithe pie." Here's how it turned out:

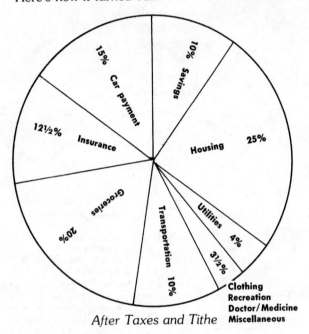

After Taxes and Tithe

This time, we ended up with 3½ per cent to cover clothing, recreation, doctor's bills, medicine and miscellaneous. There is one problem, however. By applying the 25 per cent for housing to their income after taxes and tithe, it allows only $150 for this purpose. In most areas today, this is unreal. And, trying to buy a house with this amount for a monthly payment would be practically impossible.

Our next pie consisted of the full take-home pay—after taxes. The 25 per cent for housing automatically goes up to $195—a more realistic figure. But, you will notice that we had to cut the savings to 5 per cent. This left 5½ per cent for clothing, recreation, doctor bills, medicine and miscellaneous.

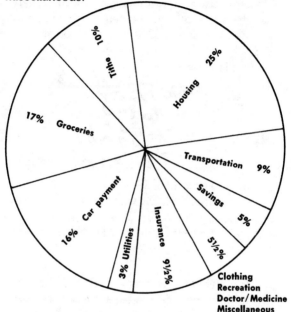

After Taxes—Net Income

It is still tight. The solution, of course, is more income. When Mike gets his next raise, it will automatically increase the amount of his taxes and tithe. However, since most entries are fixed amounts, their percentages will decrease as Mike's income increases. This will allow added percentage to go into savings.

Your percentage pie may be completely different from Mike and Lynn's, but then, no two pies are ever alike! I think you will find it interesting, though, to start with your total income and figure the per cent that goes into taxes. Then, continue with your existing expenses.

Just in case your arithmetic is a bit rusty, here is how to arrive at your percentages. If your total income per month is $900 and your food allowance is $120, just divide the larger amount into the smaller, like this:

$$
\begin{array}{r}
.13\,1/3 \\
900\,\overline{)120.00} \\
\underline{90\ 0} \\
30\ 00 \\
\underline{27\ 00} \\
3\ 00
\end{array}
$$

The answer is 13 1/3%.

I'm not sure I could live with a percentage budget, but it does offer some excellent guidelines and warnings. We'll list a few that Mike and Lynn found helpful.

1. In Exhibit #1, we discovered that 25 per cent for housing took too big a bite out of the *total income* pie. Even though a bank will approve a mortgage loan on your new home if your gross income is four times the amount of the monthly P.I.T.I. payment, it could create a tight financial position. We decided a better scale would be from 20 to 25 per cent *after* taxes.

2. We also discovered that it took 8 per cent of Mike's total wages to provide wise insurance coverage. This included medical, automobile and a conservative amount of life. As their income increases, the first two will remain

stable and they can then decide if it is time to increase the life insurance.

3. We decided that the percentages to watch and control were housing and insurance. And, the percentages to be held and protected were the tithe and savings. In the day-to-day living expenses, it would still require wise spending—and sticking to the bright red budget book!

This leaves you with the decision regarding how you figure your tithe—on income before, or after taxes. Whatever your decision, can I challenge you to put the Lord first in all of your finances? Everything you have, you have because He has made it possible. If you find that with your income and family responsibilities you can tithe your gross income, I heartily recommend it. However, if you are managing your income wisely and can't afford that amount, don't feel that less is wrong. Tithe your take-home pay and be willingly and lovingly faithful in it. You know in your heart what God expects from *you*.

CHAPTER FOURTEEN

Who Promised You a Rose Garden?

"I'm wondering just *what* it will take to upset you," Mike said with amazement, "or didn't you hear what I said?"

I had heard all right. Mike had just announced that his dental work was going to cost $3,000, and the dentist wanted cash after each session!

"Financial problems that you can't help, won't phase me," I replied calmly. "We'll work them out somehow. But, you *create* one—and you'll find out what upsets me."

We laughed, for the thought of him spending even $1 that wasn't in the budget, at that moment, seemed impossible. Outside of that one $25 dinner, he had been nearly perfect.

I was calm on the outside, but inside I was thinking, "Three thousand dollars! It's like starting all over again."

I knew that root resections, extractions, partials and caps were expensive, but I had hoped for, maybe $1,500? We would have to borrow it!

We made an appointment at the bank where they have their checking account. The gentleman we talked with didn't hold out much hope, but he gave Mike the forms to fill out and return. As we left the bank, Mike said, "It's at a time like this one could wish for a good credit rating."

There comes a time in almost everyone's life when it is necessary to borrow money. Keeping your personal finances in shape and maintaining a good credit record *are* essential. Mike was learning the hard—and embarrassing—way.

The bank, of course, turned down the loan when it received their financial statement. They were still paying on five charge accounts and one small car. However, if they could find someone who *could* qualify and who was willing to co-sign the note, they could have the money. Parents, bless them, are often lifesavers. Within a week they had their $3,000, *after* I had assured the parents that the payments on the loan would fit into the Mike and Lynn budget!

What to do with so much money? We decided to put $2,500 of it into a savings account and withdraw it as needed. It would take at least three months for the dental work to be completed. The money could earn some interest and it would also be less tempting than it would be in the checking account.

Mike would owe the $500 by next week, so this amount *was* deposited in the checking account.

Even that seemed like a fortune.

The next day, after Mike and Lynn had been to the bank, they stopped by my office. I knew at once that something was wrong. Lynn was too quiet—and Mike was too talkative! He took out his checkbook and explained a couple of small checks they had written. Just above those two checks, I noticed an unidentified entry for $9.50.

"What was the $9.50 check for?" I asked.

Lynn turned and walked away. And Mike started to explain.

"You know those free gifts the bank gives when you open a savings account? Well—we didn't like any of the free ones they had. But you could get this pocket calculator for only $9.50 extra, so I bought it."

Now, I was upset!

They didn't have $9.50 to spend. And Mike already had a pocket calculator. It had been a regular attender at every budget meeting.

For the next several minutes, I proceeded to remind Mike that buying on impulse was one of his basic problems; that he had agreed *not* to write any checks after payday without discussing it first; and—before I could offer to remove myself from his financial picture—Mike turned on his heel and walked out. Out of my office. Clear out of the building and into his car!

I felt terrible. And Lynn was crying.

"I tried to stop him from buying it," she said, "but he wouldn't listen. I cried all the way home."

That is what was bothering them when they first arrived. It was probably their first "misunderstanding," since they had gotten back together. And all over a measly $9.50!

Then I remembered.

Mike and Lynn were supposed to come to my house tomorrow night for our regular Friday budget session. Would he refuse to come? I really didn't know. He had never been angry at me before. But, then I had never bawled him out before, either.

Friday afternoon, about 3:00 P.M., Lynn called.

"What time do you want us to come tonight?" she asked.

She sounded happy. And evidently Mike was coming.

"How about seven-thirty?"

I was waiting for them when they drove up in front of the house. Mike is never at a loss for words and I wondered what his opening line would be. He didn't disappoint me!

As I opened the door, he threw his arms out wide and said, "The prodigal has returned!"

"Oh, Mike, I'd never have forgiven myself if you hadn't."

He gave me a bear hug and then, with his arm around Lynn, we all headed for the dining room. Taking his seat, Mike said, "I sold the calculator to Lynn's mom—for $9.50. We really didn't need it, nor could we afford it. It was a good lesson."

Then looking at Lynn, he added, "And, I'm sorry."

"I'm sorry, too, Mike, for losing my cool yesterday. I really don't blame you for getting angry. But I'm glad it happened. It proves that we are both human. You have been so *good* about this whole business. No one would believe you were for real if you didn't blow your top, at least once, over having someone else hold the strings on your checkbook."

He shook his head. "I don't know why I was so

determined. I guess I just wanted to spend some money on something besides bills."

"I do understand," I said, "but remember, I didn't give you all those bills. You did that all by yourselves. And besides, who promised you a rose garden?"

Lynn laughed and said, "Hey, if you do ever write a book about us, that would be a good title for one of the chapters."

Mike opened the bright red budget book. "We have to see how we are going to make the payment on our loan."

It would be six weeks before the first payment was due. Oil Company #1 would be eliminated by that time. It was going to be tight, but in just three short months the last of the seven charge accounts would be gone. After that they might even be able to double up on the loan payments once in awhile.

Mike and Lynn were going to make it. Why, this $3,000 loan didn't bother them at all. They knew how to face it and fit it into their budget. It may not be a rose garden, but it's a lot better than that patch of unruly debts they started with.

In the beginning of this book, I promised you a plan that was practical, exciting and fun. I hope you have found it to be true. I didn't, however, promise you a rose garden, either. The success of your financial recovery depends upon you. I know you can do it. Mike, Lynn and I pray that you will find some help and encouragement through their trials and triumphs and the story of their bright red budget book.

CHAPTER FIFTEEN

Now That You're Finally Out of Debt!

It would be impossible to end this book having started you on the road to recovery and not be concerned about your reaction when you are finally out of debt. There *is* a certain feeling of security in not having to make a lot of decisions regarding your money. For several months, the only decision Mike and Lynn had to make was to *stick to the budget.* And stick they did—with a healthy determination.

The controls exercised by that bright red budget book were without mercy. Don't use *even one* credit card; don't buy *anything* beyond your meager allowances; don't write checks *after* payday; pay *every* entry in that payment schedule—and on and on.

But there comes a day when the need for those restrictions is lifted. You are free! You are finally out of debt. Now, you must begin making decisions. How are you going to use that available money? Your reaction could be one of several.

You could . . .
   go beserk and start spending like
   mad;
      be afraid to spend any amount
      not listed in the bright red
      budget book;

Or, you could profit from past mistakes and exercise mature control over your future finances. And, of course, the latter is the reaction that I am hoping and praying you will have.

That bright red budget book was presented as a simple and fun way of gaining control of your runaway debts, but *you* worked it. Your assets have been faithfully used to liquidate your liabilities according to the "Payment Schedule." The "Record of Progress" was included so that you might enjoy watching your debts decline. And the list of "Goals" was planned to give you something positive to think about—something to hope for.

Now that you know how it is done, that same budget book, whatever its color might be, should remain as an effective and essential part of your family finances. You still need a twice-monthly payment schedule to control your living expenses—a plan for staying within the bounds of *your* income. And instead of listing those past due charge accounts in your "Record of Progress," you can include the monthly amounts going into those two automatic savings accounts! Watching these grow is even more fun than watching declining balances on bad debts.

When Mike and Lynn first began to have a little money left over each payday, we discussed the necessity of learning to *spend* according to priorities. The subject came up one evening after Lynn said, "I need to get some new electric curlers, or have my old ones fixed."

Then, Mike cautiously added, "And we need to replace the broken valve on our inflatable spare tire before we have another flat."

You can only put off this type of spending for so long before it catches up with you. They had been going without everything except dire emergencies for months.

I said, "Why don't you go get them?"

Lynn smiled, "It's hard to realize that we do have the money—and I guess we're just a bit afraid of starting to spend again."

A small dose of this financial fear is good for the newly recovered budgeter! Your convalescence period, however, need not be prolonged. The answer is learning to work with priorities. This is essential to good money management at any level. And it isn't nearly as limiting as it may sound.

We decided to add a page to Mike and Lynn's budget book and title it, "Needs and Wants." These should not be confused with goals although they are closely related. A goal according to Mr. Webster is, "the end toward which effort is directed." Goals are usually connected with time *and* effort—like paying bad debts or buying a house. Wants and needs fall into the category of "hair curlers" and "tire valves."

Once Mike and Lynn got started their list began to grow. This is what the first one looked like:

```
                    NEEDS AND WANTS


        NEEDS:
           Hair curlers
           Valve for tire
        Slacks
        Shoes for Mike
        Shoes for Lynn
        Tune-up for car
        New tires




        WANTS:
           New swim suit
           Day at Glenwood Springs
        New canister set
        Sports jacket
        New dress
        New tennis rackets
```

Listing needs first does not necessarily mean that all of these should be met before you can enjoy having some of your "wants." Having a list however, does let you weigh the importance of both needs and wants and determine your priorities. It helps eliminate buying on impulse. You can plan ahead and fit your spending into the most convenient payment schedule.

Mike and Lynn studied their list and decided to get the valve for the tire and the new swim suit—so they could drive to Glenwood Springs and spend the day in the pool. Even I couldn't question that decision—they deserved it! I also have confidence that in the future that list of needs will get their vote nine times out of ten.

In case you are wondering if you will ever be out of debt and have the extra money to work on a priority list, let me show you what Mike and Lynn's payment schedule will look like when they finally pay off the last charge account and that dental loan.

The rent on the new apartment was $154 and has since been raised to $185. The tithe has increased and the two savings accounts are included. When you are out of debt, take a good look at your schedule of payments used during your recovery period. Add the amounts needed to relieve any pressure points.

PAYMENT SCHEDULE		
1st of Month		40 00
Tithe		165 00
Car Payment		35 00
Savings #1		60 00
Groceries		25 00
Gasoline		11 15
Insurance		15 00
Utilities		20 00
Personal allowances		331 15
		40 00
15th of Month		185 00
Tithe		35 00
Rent		60 00
Savings #2		25 00
Groceries		8 00
Gasoline		20 00
Telephone		573 00
Personal allowances		
		800 00
Take home pay		704 15
Total expenses		95 85
Balance		

I hope and pray that you and your bright red budget book have become fast friends and that you will never be tempted to discard it in your debt-free world. Mike and Lynn join me in wishing you "happy future finances"!